PUFFIN YOUNG READERS — LEVEL 2 PROGRESSING READER

# SLOW, SLOW SLOTHS

by Bonnie Bader

Puffin Young Readers
An Imprint of Penguin Random House

Slow,

slow

sloths!

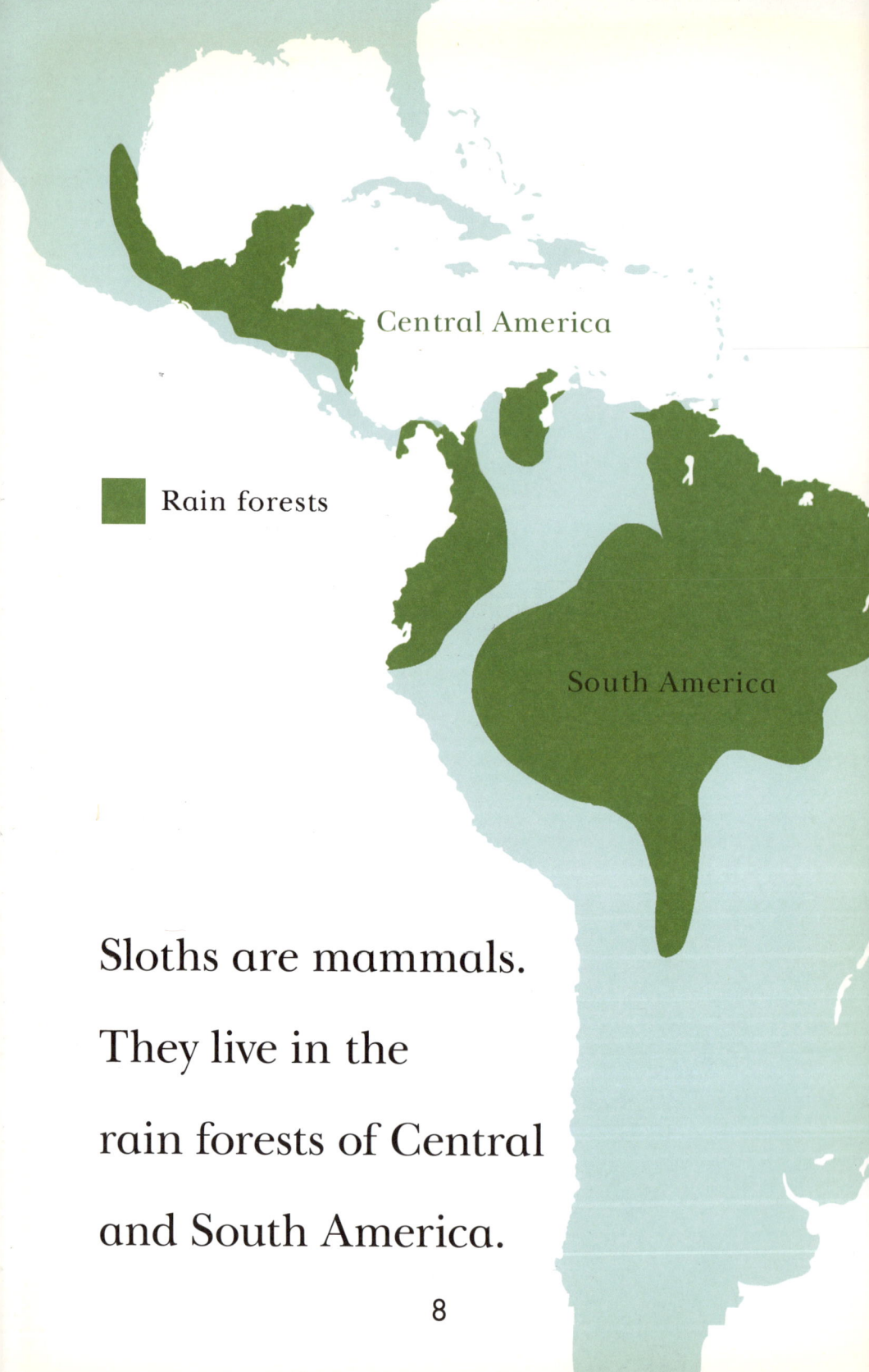

Sloths are mammals. They live in the rain forests of Central and South America.

Sloths have long arms and long fur. Are they in the same family as monkeys?

No!

Sloths are in the same family as armadillos.

# And anteaters.

There are two types of sloths.

The two-toed sloth has two claws on its front feet.

The three-toed sloth has three claws on its front feet.

All sloths have round heads.

And three- to four-inch claws.

And little ears.

And short tails.

And sad-looking eyes.

But the three-toed sloth looks like it is always smiling!

Sloths are born high up in the trees.
Baby sloths cling to their mothers' bellies until they can take care of themselves.

A young sloth likes to stay close
to its mother.
It can live with her
for up to four years.

Now it is all grown up.

It is about two feet long.

It weighs between 8 and 17 pounds.

Sloths like to live by themselves.

They sleep a lot.

Sloths sleep between 15 and 20 hours a day.

Two-toed sloths are awake at night.

Sloths hook their claws onto tree branches. They hang upside down by their long arms.

Sloths sleep and sleep and sleep.

 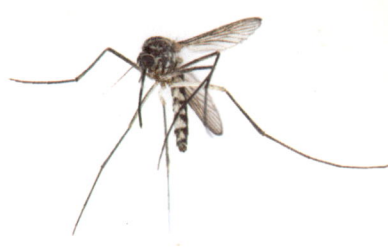

Sloths don't eat much.

They sometimes eat small insects.

Or small lizards.

But they mostly eat leaves.
Leaves do not give them
much energy.
This is one reason sloths are
so slow!

The sloth's long claws make it hard to walk on the ground. So it stays in the trees.

Some sloths stay in the same tree for years.

The only time they come down is to go to the bathroom.

Or to go for a swim.

Plop! The sloth falls from the tree into the river.

Sloths are great swimmers.

Sloths move so slowly that algae (say: AL-gee) grows on their fur. This green plant helps sloths hide from their enemies.

But they can't always hide.

Here comes a harpy eagle!

Swipe! The sloth bats at

the harpy eagle with

its long, sharp claws.

The sloth hisses.

It lets out a loud yell.

The harpy eagle flies away.

The sloth is tired

from fighting off its enemy.

It slowly climbs up the tree

and goes to sleep.

Sleep tight, slow, slow sloth!